Shell of Moon and Sun

Poems by Misuzu Kaneko

*translated
by
Yukari Meldrum
and
Alice Major*

Copyright © 2019 Alice Major and Yukari Meldrum

All rights reserved. No part of this publication may be reproduced, stored in a retrieval system, or transmitted in any form or by any means (electronic or mechanical including photocopying, recording, or any other information storage retrieval system or otherwise) without the prior written permission of the copyright owners.

For the original text, please refer to *Kaneko Misuzu Dōyō Zenshū* (Tokyo: JULA Publishing Bureau). The right to translate and publish the translation was given by the Preservation Association of Kaneko Misuzu's Literary Works.

ISBN 978-1-7907-0532-0 (pbk.)
First Edition

Cover art and design by Tiffany Adair
Book design by Yukari Meldrum

Published by Alice Major and Yukari Meldrum
P.O. Box 2108 Station Main
Edmonton, Alberta T5J 2P4
Canada

CONTENTS

Preface by Yukari Meldrum	1
Mount Ōji	4
Benten Island (Bentenjima)	5
Hanazura	6
To like everything	7
A sail	8
Me, little birds, and bells	9
Stars and dandelions	10
Dew drop	11
Spirits of flowers	12
Tsukihigai – The shell of moon and sun	13
A big haul	14
Fish	15
The Memorial Service for Whales	16
Kokoro – heart	17
At Paradise Temple	18
Hashitate's waves	19
Ōtomari Port	20
Gion Shrine	21
Komatsubara – Small pine field	22
Tree	23
Laughter	24
My hair is	25
This road	26
A note on this translation by Alice Major	28
Biography	34

Preface
by Yukari Meldrum

 I was a university student in the United States when I met Kaneko Misuzu's poetry. But first, let me introduce her.
 Kaneko Misuzu was born in 1903 and died tragically young at the age of 26. When she was 20, she started submitting her poems to various journals and continued to publish in various venues until she turned 25 when her husband forbade her to write. In her short career as a poet, she wrote 512 children's poems. Not all of them were published during her lifetime, but Misuzu gave her mentor and brother each a set of three notebooks filled with all her poems. In 1983, a children's literature scholar discovered the set of notebooks that had been given to Misuzu's brother who kept them for over 50 years. In 1984, *The Complete Works of Kaneko Misuzu* was published. Now, Misuzu's poems are loved by Japanese readers regardless of their age.
 To get back to my story, I was studying at a university in the United States to become an ESL teacher. I joined a mailing list for ESL teachers, and met a Japanese person. We became friends, discussing issues in teaching English. One day she sent me a few books as a gift, and one of the books

was a collection of poetry by Misuzu. I was mesmerized by this shiny book that was full of beautifully tender poems. Since I was starving for Japanese, whenever I had a moment, I would open the book and read whichever poem that appeared. Attending the university in English was tough for me at times, but Misuzu's poems gave me strength to move on. When I was feeling down, I would read a poem or two, and no matter what I read, I felt so much better as if some invisible hands lifted me out of a dark place.

    Misuzu's poetry is classified as children's poems in Japan. I sense that within seemingly childish and straightforward topics and themes, there exist her still-young yet adult sentiments. Her struggles with life, sadness, and tears are hidden underneath her choices of simple words. Even though her poems had this aspect, they always spoke to me with power.

    Misuzu's poems have been with me all the time. It is my hope that Alice and I are able to bring her poems to you in English in the way I have been experiencing her poems for a long time.

Mount Ōji

The cherry trees, planted on this hillside
to make it into a park, have withered.

But stumps of old, not-so-important trees
are bushy with green shoots.

Silver ocean shines between trees.
There my town floats just like
the dragon god's palace.

Silver roof tiles and stone walls
look hazy, dream-like.

When I look down from Mount Ōji,
I grow fonder of this town.

The smell of fish fertilizer never reaches here.
Only the fragrance of new green.

Benten Island (Bentenjima)

"So cute a little island
should be somewhere else.
I'll drag it away with a rope."

This is what the laughing sailor said,
the one who came from the north.

No! No! I thought. That night was dark
and I lay worried.

The morning came up – I ran with my heart
going thumpty-thump, all the way to the shore.

But Benten Island lay
on the waves,
wrapped in gold light,
green as ever.

Hanazura

Once upon a time, at the shore
near Hanazura, I heard
"Once upon a time…"
And now when I see
the great rock of Hanazura,
I remember with a lonely heart.

Once upon a time,
the tale of Hanazura was told to me
by the man from the post office.
And I wonder now, where is he?

Ships have disappeared
around the edge
of Hanazura.

Now the ocean flames at sunset.
Now ships still journey away.

Once upon a time. And time,
oh Hanazura, has taken all away.

To like everything

I want to become a person
who likes everything and anything.

Even onions, even tomatoes, even fish,
to like everything with nothing left out.

In our house, all the bowls of food
are made by our mother.

I want to become a person
who likes everyone and anyone.

Even going to see a doctor and even crows,
to like everyone with no one left out.

In this world, all of its many things
are made by our gods.

A sail

For just a sec
I looked at a seashell on the beach.
And that sail
disappeared.

Just in this way,
      withdrawn –
Someone has gone
Something has gone.

Me, little birds, and bells

Even if I spread my arms out wide,
I can't fly high in the sky. But,
the little birds that do can't really run
fast the way I can.

Even if I wriggle my body around,
I can't make beautiful ringing. But,
the bells that ring can't really sing
all the songs that I know.

Bells, little birds, and I –
we're all different and we're all fine.

Stars and dandelions

Deep, deep at the bottom of the blue sky,
like tiny pebbles on the floor of the sea,
they stay there until the night.
You can't see stars in the sun.
    You cannot see them, but they're there.
    Things you can't see are actually there.

Dandelions wilted and died
quietly between the paving stones.
You cannot see their strong roots.
They hide until spring comes.
    You cannot see them, but they're there.
    Things you can't see are actually there.

Dew drop

I won't tell
anyone that

in the morning
down in the little corner of the yard
the flower cried a little tear.

If the rumor spread wide
and the bee heard about it,

he would go return the nectar
as if he'd done
something bad.

Spirits of flowers

Spirits of flowers that died
will all be reborn
in Buddha's garden.

Because they are kind.
When the sun calls them,
they pop open and smile.
They give sweet juices to butterflies
and give us all the nice smell.

When the winds call them,
they follow happily.

Even their bodies can be
plates of food when we play house.

Tsukihigai – The shell of moon and sun

The scarlet of sky in the west
the red sun under the sea.
In the east of the sky, our moon
is a round and creamy pearl.

The sun that goes down at sunset.
The moon that sinks down at dawn.
They meet on the deep floor of sea.

One day, a fisherman finds
a shell of deep red
and pale yellow.

A big haul

Ships in the glowing sunrise.
A big haul,
Ōba sardines in the holds,
a big haul.

On the shore, it looks like
the shine of a festival,
but under the water
how many funerals?

Fish

Oh, the poor fish from the sea.

People raise rice.
People ranch cows.
Even carp in the ponds,
we feed them.

But fish from the sea,
No one feeds them.
They don't act bad.
But still, here they are
flat on my plate.

Poor, poor fish from the sea.

The Memorial Service for Whales

The service for whales is held in late spring
around the season when flying fish are caught at sea.

When the ringing of the bell from the temple on the shore
carries across the surface of the water,

when the village fishermen wear their good jackets
over kimonos, and hurry to the temple on the shore,

out at sea, a lonely whale child
listens to the ringing of the bell,

and cries – *You are dead, mother, father,
I miss you, I miss you.*

How far on the water's wide surface,
how far will the bell's echo go?

Kokoro – heart

My mother is a grown-up,
and she is big,
but her heart is little,

because my mother says
it's all filled up with me.

I am a kid,
and I am small,
but my heart is big,

because my big mother
does not quite fill it all the way,
and I have room for lots of other stuff.

At Paradise Temple

At the temple, there are cherries, double flowering,
– double-flowering –
I saw them when I went to run an errand.

When I turned at the corner of the side street,
when I turned,
I saw them from the corner of my eyes.

At the temple, cherry trees on the bare ground,
– the bare ground –
blooming, blooming from the ground.

Carrying a wakame rice ball for my lunch,
for my lunch,
we went back to see the cherry trees in flower.

Hashitate's waves

Hashitate's waves come over, come over.
In the lake to the right, the grebes dive under,
                              dive under.
On the sea to the left, white sails sail by.
And through the pine woods of Komatsubara
the whoosh whoosh of light wind blows over.
   the sea gulls   play
   with the ducks of the lake   all day
   when the blue moon   comes out
   the lake spirit wanders   to look for shells
   on the shore
Hashitate's waves come over, come over.
On the right, small waves chuckle, yes.
On the left, sea waves thunder, yes.
On the land, the small stones of Koishihara
click clack under wooden sandals.
        You can't come over.

Ōtomari Port

On my way from the mountain festival,
after Aunty saw me part way home,
and I was walking down from the pass,
I saw the lovely sea glitter
through cedar branches.

On the sea, a boat's still sail,
on the shore a glimpse of red straw roofs –
as though everything is in the sky,
as though everything is in a dream.

At the foot of the pass is a buckwheat field,
and at the end of the field,
I see Ōtomari. Once, its name meant big
but oh, today,
the port is old and lonely.

Gion Shrine

Softly and quietly
pine needles are falling.
Autumn at the temple grounds
is a little lonely.

Last season, the songs
of children's shows –
dancing dolls in boxes.
The flames of gas lamps.
The cinnamon trees with red belts.

Now, only
the crumbling shaved-ice stand,
gently swept
by autumn's breath.

Komatsubara – Small pine field

In Komatsubara,
there aren't as many pine trees.

An old woodcutter is always
sawing the big timbers,

pushing and pulling. With every stroke
a distant white sail shows itself, then hides.

Over the waves fly the gulls.
In the sky the larks cry.

It is spring in the sea and the sky,
but the pine trees and woodman look lonesome.

Here and there
new houses are popping up.
There are fewer pine trees in
Komatsubara.

Tree

Flowers fall, and
fruits ripen.

The fruits fall, and
the leaves, too.

Then, buds come out, and
flowers bloom.

How often will
the tree continue
through this circle
before her work is done?

Laughter

It is the beautiful color of roses.
Smaller than poppy seeds, but when
it cascades to the ground,
giant flowers burst out,
    just like fireworks.

If laughter could spill like this
    as easily as tears spill
how lovely, lovely it would be.

My hair is

My hair is shiny because
my mom always strokes it.

My nose is a bit flat because
I make noises for fun.

My apron is white because
my mom always washes it.

My skin is rather dark because
I snack on roasted soybeans.

This road

Further along this road
there must be a very big forest.
Oh, lonely hackberry tree,
let's go down this path.

Further along this road
there must be a large sea.
Mr. Frog of the lotus pond,
let's go down this path.

Further along this road
there must be a busy city.
Oh, scarecrow, looking lonely,
let's go down this path.

There must be something, something
further along this road.
Everyone, everyone, let's go down this path.

A note on this translation
By Alice Major

Working with Yukari Meldrum to recreate these poems in English made me very aware of the three separate strands that must be braided together in translation. First and obviously, there is rendering the meaning of words — not simply their literal meaning, but their nuance and emotional connotation. Then there is the attention to sound: what kind of patterns does the original poem make, and how can you echo them? Finally, there is the context, the world in which the poem was created.

For me, this was an opportunity to learn a little bit about the structure and poetic traditions of a language that is so very different from my own. Misuzu's poems were composed by a very young woman from a world that was beginning to vanish. She was born in fishing village in a remote part of Japan, a world of sea-related ceremonies, temple bells, and a belief system amalgamating Shinto gods and Buddhism. She also stood at the cusp of change in the 1920s, where she could begin to connect with a new urban community of writers and editors but where she could be married off to a man who would forbid her to do so.

These poems have a special fragrance, a gentle pot-pourri. They come from a particular time and place that seems both distant and close: a seaside town in the early part of the twentieth century, rituals of fishing and temple, a child hearing scraps of conversation, a culture that valued restraint over turmoil and adventure. (The closest thing I can think of in English literature comes in the narrative viewpoint of certain novels by Jane Gardham.)

As translators, we are trying to create a braid strong enough to pull this whole world through a keyhole. To do so, we pondered numerous choices of phrase and diction. For instance, we wanted to incorporate the details of Japanese culture without making them overly exotic; in the original, these details are simply part of everyday life. So, for example in *The Memorial Service for Whales*, we translated 'haori,' (a kind of formal clothing worn over a full-length kimono-like garment on special occasions) as "good jackets over kimonos" because 'kimono' is a term that is familiar enough in English and still carries the sense of Japanese culture in the translation.

Misuzu's poems were not written in the classic forms of Japanese poetry—they are often looser, more 'modern' in shape—but they preserve the traditional underlying beat of 5-7-5 syllables, an unconscious counting that tells the listener that language is being used in a special way. We chose not to try to replicate the syllable count of lines, since syllables in English are defined much less clearly and consistently than in Japanese. We retained features like stanza lengths and overall shape, with Misuzu's line indentations. But often we turned to the closest equivalent to the 5-7-5 pattern in English poetry, which is the iambic rhythm of stressed/unstressed syllables that creates the heartbeat of poetry in this language.

And, although Misuzu's poems are often considered 'for children,' we did not turn to the common English convention of rhyming used in verse for young readers. Writing poetry for children was taken seriously by well established, highly regarded authors. The voice in her work may often be child-like, but it is never childish. Her poems are for wise, observant children, who may be occasionally and quietly rebellious but are conscious (in a very Japanese way) of the duty not to burden others—flowers that do not want to make a bee feel badly by shedding a tear-like drop of dew. They are children who empathize with the whale-child whose parents have been caught by fishermen. They notice the dreamy light on roof-tops.

We made many careful choices as we tried to braid the three strands of emotional significance, sound and context. As just a few examples:

In *Memorial Service for Whales*, the word 'koishi' is an adjective in Japanese which cannot be translated directly into English. It expresses a full range of strong emotions, a longing for someone who is not present or far away. We might have used a term like 'heartbroken' but that didn't approach the direct simplicity we needed. This is a child's experience of loss, so we used "I miss you," and depended on the context provided by the narrative situation to give the words their impact.

Benten Island is a small narrative from the child's point of view. Rather than trying to stick to the literal translation, we tried to convey her feelings closely as possible. The third stanza starts with "Uso da, uso da," which literally translates as "It's a lie, it's a lie." What might an English-speaking child say? We thought that a direct expression of "No! No!" would fit here well to express how worried this child was feeling – a pure sense of denial.

Japanese often use onomatopoeic expressions, and in this poem, too, we have one: "dokidoki" in the fourth stanza. This is a sound of the heart beating. Luckily for us, there is an almost-exact English equivalent, "thumpty-thump".

In *Sails*, the colours "kuro" and "shiro" can be literally translated as "black" and "white." However, the binary opposition of black and white is too harsh and carries too many other connotations in English. Misuzu's original suggests that the sails have been blackened, or dirtied, in the course of their lives through many journeys, so we decided to use "dirtied sails" instead of "black."

The very last line of *Hanazura* in the original is "minna mukashi ni narimashita" which literally translates into "all have become past." The original line sounds as if it is the end of the tale, pulling the curtains down at the end of the play. To convey the strong emotion that something has actively been lost, we translated the lines as "time […] has taken all away."

In *Stars and Dandelions*, the fourth line of the original is "hiru no ohoshi," which literally means "daytime stars." Our translation as "stars in the sun" gives the pleasure of alliteration in English, but also echoes the fact that the word for "day" in Japanese ("hi" or "nichi") is represented by a character that incorporates the concept of sun.

The main work of translation was carried out by Yukari, who brought her own native understanding of Japanese speaking patterns and culture. I simply brought my own experience of poetry in English to help. It was a privilege to do so. In that process, this small collection of translated poems became, for me, a glimpse through a window, beckoning. As Kaneko Misuzu wrote,

There must be something, something
further along this road.
Everyone, everyone, let's go down this path.

Biography

Alice Major

Alice Major has published 11 collections of poetry and a book of essays on poetry and science. Her work has won many awards, including the 2017 Lieutenant Governor of Alberta Distinguished Artist Award. She is the founder of the Edmonton Poetry Festival. *www.alicemajor.com*.

Yukari Meldrum

Yukari is a translator, interpreter, and poet. A translation book *Will not forget both laughter and tears* written by Tomoko Mitani was published by the University of Alberta Press in 2013. A poetry-and-art collaborative book *Somnio: the way we see it* was published together with Tiffany Adair, Pushpa Acharya, and Sharmila Pokharel in 2015. Yukari also spends a lot of her time sewing and making things with her hands. *www.yukarimeldrum.com*

Milton Keynes UK
Ingram Content Group UK Ltd.
UKHW011310201223
434718UK00005B/428